BIGGEST NAMES IN SPORTS
MIKE TROUT

BASEBALL STAR

by Matt Tustison

FOCUS
READERS

WWW.FOCUSREADERS.COM

Focus Readers is distributed by North Star Editions:
sales@northstareditions.com | 888-417-0195

Produced for Focus Readers by Red Line Editorial.

Photographs ©: Peter Joneleit/Cal Sport Media/AP Images, cover, 1; Jeff Roberson/AP Images, 4–5, 9; Paul Sancya/AP Images, 7; Seth Poppel/Yearbook Library, 10–11; Rich Schultz/AP Images, 13; Jae C. Hong/AP Images, 15; Matt A. Brown/AP Images, 16–17; Tony Gutierrez/AP Images, 18; Patrick Smith/Reuters/Newscom, 21; Chris Carlson/AP Images, 22–23; John Cordes/Icon Sportswire/AP Images, 24; Chris Williams/Icon Sportswire/AP Images, 27; Red Line Editorial, 29

ISBN
978-1-63517-490-8 (hardcover)
978-1-63517-562-2 (paperback)
978-1-63517-706-0 (ebook pdf)
978-1-63517-634-6 (hosted ebook)

Library of Congress Control Number: 2017948072

Printed in the United States of America
Mankato, MN
November, 2017

ABOUT THE AUTHOR

Matt Tustison is a sports copy editor at the *Washington Post*. He also has worked as a sports copy editor at other newspapers, including the *Baltimore Sun*, and as an editor and writer of children's sports books.

TABLE OF CONTENTS

CHAPTER 1

A STAR AMONG STARS

The 2014 All-Star Game had just begun. Suddenly, the sound of the ball hitting the bat echoed throughout the stadium. Mike Trout of the American League (AL) had just connected off National League (NL) pitcher Adam Wainwright. It was a first-inning drive to right field.

Trout takes a mighty swing at the 2014 All-Star Game.

The ball went over the head of the leaping right fielder. Then it bounced off the bottom of the 23-foot (7.0-m) wall. The AL's Derek Jeter ran home easily from second base, scoring the game's first run. Meanwhile, Trout raced around the bases. He slid into third for a triple. Trout looked

PASSING THE TORCH

The 2014 All-Star Game was the final All-Star Game for Derek Jeter. He would be retiring at season's end. The New York Yankees' shortstop was Trout's hero when Trout was growing up in New Jersey. Trout played shortstop and wore No. 2 on his uniform as a kid. That was Jeter's number. As Jeter was finishing his incredible career, a new "face of baseball" was emerging in Trout.

Trout talks to Derek Jeter during a warm-up before the game.

into the AL dugout and clapped his hands. In one play, the Los Angeles Angels' star had shown off his tremendous power and speed.

But Trout wasn't done. In the bottom of the fifth inning, he came to bat again. The score was tied 3–3. Runners were at first and second with one out. Trout chopped the ball down the line and past the NL third baseman. The AL's Derek Norris scored from second for the go-ahead run. Trout ran into second base for a double.

The AL went on to win the game 5–3. Trout was only 22 years old. But he was already appearing in his third All-Star Game. This time he was named the game's most valuable player (MVP). On one of the biggest stages in Major League Baseball (MLB), Mike Trout was the brightest star.

Trout shows off his MVP trophy after the game.

CHAPTER 2

THE EARLY YEARS

Mike Trout was born on August 7, 1991. He grew up in southern New Jersey, about 50 miles (80 km) from Philadelphia, Pennsylvania. Mike loved baseball from a young age. He was a big fan of the Philadelphia Phillies.

Mike wanted to play catch all the time. Sometimes he even slept in his uniform.

Mike was the star of his high school baseball team.

He learned how to play from his father, who had been a minor league infielder.

Mike played baseball and basketball at Millville High School. At first, he was a pitcher and a shortstop. But during his senior year, he moved to the outfield. Mike hit 18 home runs that season, setting a state record. Outside of high school, he also played baseball on a traveling team.

Mike graduated from high school in 2009. He had size, speed, and power. This combination was rare in young **prospects**. The Los Angeles Angels selected him in the first round of the 2009 MLB **draft**.

Mike was only 17 years old when the Angels drafted him.

Mike chose to start his pro career right away instead of attending college. His Angels **contract** included a signing bonus of more than $1 million.

Trout began his minor league career in the **rookie**-level Arizona League. He played very well, so the Angels **promoted** him. Soon he was playing for the Cedar Rapids Kernels in the Class A Midwest League.

Trout started the 2010 season at Cedar Rapids. And he continued to **excel**. That July, he was chosen to play in MLB's All-Star Futures Game. The game is for talented prospects, and it was held in Anaheim, California. Trout batted well and scored twice as the US team beat the World team 9–1.

The Angels were impressed with Trout's performance. The team promoted him to

Trout attempts to steal a base in the All-Star Futures Game in 2010.

the Rancho Cucamonga Quakes of the Class A-Advanced California League. He hit .306 in 50 games for the Quakes. Following the season, Trout was named the 2010 Topps Minor League Player of the Year. And he was only 19 years old.

CHAPTER 3

A BIG HIT IN THE MAJORS

In 2011, Mike Trout began the season with the Arkansas Travelers of the Class AA Texas League. Before long, the Angels promoted Trout to the majors. The **phenom** made his big league debut on July 8, 2011. The next night, in a game against the Seattle Mariners, Trout had a bunt single. It was his first MLB hit.

Trout fields a ball in his first major league game.

Trout rounds the bases during a win over the Texas Rangers in 2011.

Trout went back and forth between the majors and Class AA in 2011. In all, he played 40 games for Los Angeles. He batted only .220 and hit five homers. But in the minors, Trout dominated in

91 games for Arkansas. *Baseball America* named him 2011 Minor League Player of the Year.

The youngster started the 2012 season with the Class AAA Salt Lake Bees. Trout excelled, and it didn't take long for the Angels to call him up. This time, he would stay in the majors for good.

Trout was officially a rookie in 2012. And he had one of the best rookie seasons ever. He hit .326 with 30 homers. Trout led the AL with 129 runs scored and 49 steals. The center fielder showed that he had many talents. He could hit for average and for power. He could field and throw well. And he had great speed.

The Angels finished third in their division. But Trout was **unanimously** named the AL Rookie of the Year. At 21 years old, he was the youngest player ever to win the award. Trout also finished second in the AL MVP race.

In 2013, Trout again placed second for AL MVP. This time he batted .323 with

GREAT WITH THE GLOVE

In his rookie season of 2012, Trout demonstrated his tremendous defensive ability. On June 27, he leaped at the wall in center field to rob the Baltimore Orioles' J. J. Hardy of a home run. Trout checked his glove to make sure the ball was still there. When he saw it, he flashed a big smile.

Trout makes a spectacular grab to prevent a home run.

27 homers. He led the AL in runs with 109 and walks with 110. He also showed his speed by stealing 33 bases. Even so, the Angels finished a disappointing third place in their division.

CHAPTER 4

STREAKING TO FAME

Mike Trout was already a rising star, but 2014 was his best year yet. In March, the Angels signed him to a contract extension. He would make $144.5 million over six years. Trout then led the AL in runs and runs batted in (RBIs).

Trout celebrates a game-winning home run against the Tampa Bay Rays in 2014.

Trout sprints to second base after his teammate hits a ground ball.

More important, the Angels won their division. For the first time in Trout's career, he had made it to the postseason. Los Angeles faced the Kansas City Royals in the AL Division Series. Trout hit a home run in Game 3 of the series, but it wasn't enough. The Angels lost to the Royals in a three-game **sweep**.

After the season was over, Trout was unanimously chosen as the AL MVP for the 2014 season. He became only the sixth player to win the regular-season and All-Star Game MVP awards in the same season.

In 2015, Trout picked up right where he left off. He smashed a career-high 41 homers. He also became the first player ever to win the All-Star Game MVP award in two straight years. He led off the game with an opposite-field homer off NL pitcher Zack Greinke. Trout scored twice in the AL's 6–3 win.

However, the Angels failed to reach the postseason. The team's struggles continued in 2016. Even so, Trout had another amazing year. He led the league in runs and walks. He also slugged 29 homers and had 100 RBIs. Trout's impressive season earned him his second MVP award.

A CHARITY ALL-STAR

Off the field, Trout has gotten involved in many charities. One of them is Big Brothers Big Sisters. The organization provides mentoring to young people who are dealing with difficult life circumstances. Trout also has visited sick children in hospitals and helped raised funds for at-risk youth.

Trout speaks to the crowd while accepting the second MVP award of his career.

Despite the Angels' struggles, people continued going out to the ballpark in 2017. They wanted to see Trout and his unique combination of skills. Fans everywhere agreed that Trout was one of the best baseball players in the world.

MIKE TROUT

- Height: 6 feet 2 inches (188 cm)
- Weight: 235 pounds (107 kg)
- Birth date: August 7, 1991
- Birthplace: Vineland, New Jersey
- High school: Millville High School (Millville, New Jersey)
- Minor league teams: Cedar Rapids Kernels (2009), Rancho Cucamonga Quakes (2010), Arkansas Travelers (2011), Salt Lake Bees (2012)
- MLB teams: Los Angeles Angels (2011–)
- Major awards: AL MVP (2014, 2016), AL Rookie of the Year (2012)

Salt Lake City

Los Angeles

Cedar Rapids

Millville

Rancho Cucamonga

Little Rock

FOCUS ON
MIKE TROUT

Write your answers on a separate piece of paper.

1. Write a sentence that describes the main ideas of Chapter 2.

2. Do you think Trout would be a better player if he had played baseball in college? Why or why not?

3. What was Trout's favorite team when he was growing up?

    A. Seattle Mariners
    B. Los Angeles Angels
    C. Philadelphia Phillies

4. How did Trout's dad help make him a better baseball player?

    A. He took Mike to lots of Phillies games.
    B. He played baseball in the minors and taught Mike to play.
    C. He gave Mike money to attend college.

Answer key on page 32.

GLOSSARY

contract
An agreement to pay someone a certain amount of money.

draft
A system that allows teams to acquire new players coming into a league.

excel
To do extremely well.

phenom
A young person who is very talented.

promoted
Moved someone up to a higher level.

prospects
Players who are likely to be successful in the future.

rookie
A professional athlete in his or her first year.

sweep
Winning all of the games in a series.

unanimously
When everyone agrees on something.

TO LEARN MORE

BOOKS

Morreale, Marie. *Mike Trout*. New York: Scholastic, 2016.

Nelson Maurer, Tracy. *Mike Trout*. North Mankato, MN: Capstone Press, 2016.

Robinson, Tom. *Today's 12 Hottest MLB Superstars*. Mankato, MN: 12-Story Library, 2015.

WEBSITES

Visit **www.focusreaders.com** to find lesson plans, activities, links, and other resources related to this title.

INDEX

Answer Key: 1. Answers will vary; **2.** Answers will vary; **3.** C; **4.** B